Poetry for Lovers

Poetry for Lovers

by
Maxine Daniels

Editor & Proofreader
Kurt Conrad
Antonia M. Gaskin

Photography by
Brian Everest
(Everest Design Ltd)

Senior Publisher
Steven Lawrence Hill Sr.

Awarded Publishing House
ASA Publishing Company
Established Since 2005

A Publisher Trademark Copy page

ASA Publishing Company
Awarded Best Publisher for Quality Books 2008, 2009
Nominated for the Better Business Bureau 2012 Torch Award
105 E. Front St., Suite 101, Monroe, Michigan 48161
United States of America
www.asapublishingcompany.com

All Rights Reserved. No part of this publication may be reproduced, stored in a retrieval system or transmitted in any form or by any means electronic, mechanical, photocopying, recording, taping, web distribution, information storage, or otherwise, without the prior written permission of the publisher. Author/writer rights to "Freedom of Speech" protected by and with the "1st Amendment" of the Constitution of the United States of America. This poetry is a work of fiction spoken in an American, British, and French combined languages that can be used for educational and historical learning purposes. With this title page, the reader is notified that the publisher does not assume, and expressly disclaims any obligation to obtain and/or include any other information other than that provided by the author. Any belief system, promotional motivations, including but not limited to the use of non-fiction characters and/or characteristics of this book, are within the boundaries of the author's own creativity and/or testimony in order to reflect the nature and concept of the book.

Any and all vending sales and distribution not permitted without full book cover and this title page.

Copyrights©2013 Maxine Daniels, All Rights Reserved
Book: Poetry for Lovers
Date Published: 02.13.2012
Edition: 1 *Trade Paperback*
Book ASAPCID: 2380600
ISBN: 978-1-886528-54-3
Library of Congress Cataloging-in-Publication Data

This book was published in the United States of America.
State of Michigan

A Publisher Trademark Title page

PART 1

Love	…………...	7
The Wait	…………...	9
Time	…………...	10
Look at Me	…………...	11
The Wind of Change	…………...	12
Rise Above	…………...	13
Children Belong to Themselves	…………...	14
The Mind Questions	…………...	15
Ode to a Drunk	…………...	16
Breadth of Vision	…………...	17

PART II

Dreams	…………...	18
My Prayer	…………...	19
Given Sight	…………...	20
To You My Father	…………...	21
Lovers Lament	…………...	22
First Love	…………...	23
Haunting Flight	…………...	25
To Know Love	…………...	26

PART III

What's in a Name	…………...	27

Listen to the Look	…………...	28
Destiny	…………...	30
Unselfish Thoughts	…………...	32
Insecurity	…………...	34
Presence Accepted	…………...	35
Resentment	…………...	36
When	…………...	37
A Voice From Above	……………..	38
Hurt	……………..	40
Warm	……………..	41
Abandoned	……………..	42
Warmth Froze	……………..	45
Dwell in a Dream	……………..	46
Home	……………..	47

PART IV

Talk	……………..	48
Look of Change	……………..	49
Passed By	……………..	50
Feelings Stirred	……………..	51
A Glint	……………...	53
Tears	……………...	54

Do You Remember	…………..	55
Christmas Sharing	…………..	57

PART V

Faith	…………..	58
Awakening	…………..	59
Thought	…………..	60
Uplifted	…………..	61
Materialism	…………..	62
Melting	…………..	63
Hello You	…………..	64
Harmony	…………..	65
Jewel	…………..	66
Missing Loving	…………..	67
Voila!	…………..	69
A Breeze	…………..	70
Cold Memories	…………..	71
Love	…………..	72
Friend	…………..	73
Think Before You Speak	…………..	74
Old Flame	…………..	75
The End is the Beginning	…………..	76
Alone	…………..	77

Hurt 78
Lovebirds 79

Poetry for Lovers
by Maxine Daniels

*LOVE IS SHARING THIS LIFE TOGETHER
IF IT BE FOREVER, SO LET IT BE
UNTIL THE TIDE OF TIME FLOODS THE SHORE
AND TOGETHERNESS IS SHARED NO MORE*

ASA Publishing Company

PART I

LOVE

I wrote last night of past feelings,
I write tonight of how I see things,
The past has brought me up to date,
My brain's been fed, I'm wide-awake

I know what life is all about,
I haven't time for wasters
How strange you thought the same as I
A sentence said, it clears my head,
You smile, you say,
A few words a day, so my fear surpasses,
I hear your words,
I see your smile

I trust in your advances,
I like the way you share your day,
I am happy living this way.

I'd like to think there is more in store,
That you could love me more and more,
I need your love, I need to know,
I'm insecure, yes I know

In the past,
I've ignored the glance of men in all their splendor,
Compliments, I seem to dread,
Their sentiment never tender,
I've been hurt, haven't we all,
My hurt though exceptionally cruel,
So give me time, my own sweet love
And engulf me in your love………

I'm halfway there,
I know you care,
But I'm frightened of the Lion's lair.
I want to love, with total trust,
And to know that we will always be

I want us to be as one,
Our love to shine,
Like the midday sun,
I never thought I would feel this way,
I love you more than words can say,

Please, don't ever go away.

THE WAIT

A dripping tap, a ticking clock,
The fridge going on and off,
My heart is pounding, missing beats -
Do or die, I think I'll cry -
If he turns *left*, *my heart* will shred.

If he turns *right*, what is my plight?
I do not know,
If his love will grow or even if it's there
Could he, can he, does he
Know *how much* I CARE?

Could he, can he, will he, ever really love me?
Trust my love for I'll be true,
I've waited such a long time for you.

TIME

Time to heal a broken heart,
To mend a rift - time apart,
For love to grow to understand,
A babe in arms, time plays its hand.

When time runs out - how shallow life,
The past, the present, where was life?
How quickly one forgets to breathe,
When pain beseeches thee and seethes,
Life is like a highway road
It has its light it has its code.

Time plays a waiting game it brings you joy,
A world of knowledge, you store that time,
Like a computer fed,
Until God says, and so to bed,
To sleep the sleep of peace and dream
Of how, *life* might have been.

Perhaps one day,
You may return to start afresh,
To yearn, one does not fear the sleep in store,
Just the time when one wants more,
And in your heart you know when,
You'll never see the dawn again.

LOOK AT ME

Love of life, live to love,
Peace in the form of a dove,
Golden silence, peace of mind,
Words of a different kind

Do you understand? Are you understood?
Would words make it easier?
Only if spoken with sentiment and truth
Could words make life simple?

An element of proof
To say that you care,
Three words people dare to utter,
Really without a thought,
For it is not the words they say
But how they plan and share their day,
A meeting perchance a loving glance
A warmth no words can say.

It's in a smile, eyes hold a glow,

You know, you just know.

THE WIND OF CHANGE

These thoughts of a different kind,
They are changes, in my mind,
The real me is coming through,
Deep, complexed, wondering what will happen next?
Part of me is still quite blue,
But the inner me has a warm tranquility.

As I expand mentally, my memory,
That has hurt so bitterly, now has shades of gray,
In the past it was black all day.
I wonder if people will know
That calmness within flows,
For the joy of a woman
Is the contentment she feels inside.
It is the one emotion her face cannot hide,
If it comes with the knowledge
Of how to love and be loved,
Then I have found my longing,
But, I feel it comes with a sense of belonging.

RISE ABOVE

The Telegram arrived,
Such a sweet refrain,
Phone the bungalow, Oh no not again,
All of a quiver, I did as I was bid.

The shouting, the screaming,
A man so deceiving-How does a Father behave?
This one my friend, (I refer to my pen),
would like me in my grave.

Well I'm not going I said and promptly went,
To bury my feet in the sand with Telegram in hand
Scattered pieces to sea!!

No tears for me at the end of the day,
Sorry folks didn't end that way.
On again to a so-called *Friend*, "Don't want to know", she uttered to me,
Up in the clouds went my head,
To the mountains I sped,
I'm not upside down I'm firm on the ground.
Why can't "anyone" see?

CHILDREN BELONG TO THEMSELVES

Children are borrowed,
A weekend,
A day,
When they're grown
Do they stay?
Your job to put them on their merry way,
Teach right from wrong,
Sing a song,
Play the music,
Wonder what went wrong,
Nothing Dad, Nothing Mum,
I just cannot sing your song!

I am me thanks to thee
And will live my life as I see fit!
I have the advantage,
The right kit,
Thanks to you,
You saw me through,
Love was all you had to do,
Right from wrong.
I'll learn as I go along,
But I have to sing my own song,
I'll look back in years and shed tears!
As I watch my offspring sing their song.

THE MIND QUESTIONS

Difficult to answer, the questions you ask yourself,
View life as though it were a shelf,
Take your pick not too quick
See how it's made,
Plastic or wood,
Marble or stone,
People are capable of shading their tones,
Which ones are stable?
Wood or stone.
How are you able to detect undertones?
You can't.
That is why you ask of yourself,
Your conscience pricks
Because something doesn't tick
In the person you are viewing as the shelf,
When it clicks the shelf unfixed
It's not a person you want around,
Have you answered the question as to why this is so,
Difficult to answer, but you know that it's No!

ODE TO A DRUNK

Take me back, the drunkard said,
What was going through his head
"I hit because I love you,"
How can that be, when logic has ceased
The alcohol dims the brain,
Only his victim feels the pain,
I've aged years and shake with fear.

Will his fist take aim again,
He cannot remember when,
He broke my ribs or bruised my face,
He only knows the liquor taste.

He is beyond help what's left now,
A church and steeple?
No, bar flies die, inside they're dead,
All that's left is the body to shed,
Bury him, don't dare,
Cremate him, sift the ashes into a bottle,
Leave it in some bar,
So he can watch brandy from afar.

BREADTH OF VISION

Decisions, Decisions, What to do?
I'm beginning to feel like a pair of shoes,
Now think of that, they don't walk back,
They go one in front of the other,
Some shine, some climb,
They're comfortable though under your toes,
On the floor - you walk to open the door,
Turn to re-enter should you venture?

Look at nature, nothing greater,
Trees have roots and offshoots,
Birds take flight not knowing their plight,
The peace of the dove not cupboard love,
Man must expand, he has plans,
Grasp for the wings of the dove,
Peace of mind, its unkind
Perhaps it doesn't come with love,
Work to rule that's cruel,
Man must be free like the wind in the trees
And the ever-flowing sea!

PART II

DREAMS

As you lay asleep in bed,
Let the fairies take your head
The stars will light the way so bright,
Like a bird, taking flight,
Off you will go to lands afar,
Mystical, Magical, follow the star,
Yesterday, yesteryear, your future now so very clear,
The dreams you had whilst on your feet,
You only got there when asleep,
Then one day you stopped to say,
This is life, I like it this way.

The dreams you dreamt, were not so far,
The light of life, your shining star,
Awake or asleep, it's yours to keep,
Reach out and touch,
Dreams mean so much,
They're in your head when you're in bed,
Your conscience coming through,
Til in the end, you *wake* my friend
And find the real you!

MY PRAYER

In the Lord above
I place my love
My trust and my life
For he will guide me
Where he wants me to be
The Lord is with me
I believe in Thee

That prayer came from the depths of my soul
My body then was not whole
Love of life for me had gone
In my heart was a different song
Tired of living
Given up hope
Things I wanted were so remote
Sleepless nights drifting days
Life a mere existence

Hands grasped tightly
Looking up at the night
I stood and said with all my heart
"Dear Lord, it's time for me to part."
I remember well
That very night
T'was on that night
That I did write My Prayer

Voiced in times of fear
When I need a guiding light
I thank thee Lord
For sending me those words
They are my life's light - My prayer.

GIVEN SIGHT

For a living I'm a sage
That doesn't come with age
It's a gift you see
From the powers that be

Now and again the telephone rings
A smiling voice relates good things
That have been bestowed
When at the time of my seeing them
They were full of woe
But I have faith and trust in my teachers
They know what will happen and how
I merely interpret their every vow

Relating their wishes
With warmth and love
Calming rough feathers with peace from above
Seeing their path guided by light
Taking that person through the depths of their plight
Having the faith to know it's right

Such was today
A man telephoned to say
His fortune had changed
Life was re-arranged
Thanking me he rang off with glee
But of course it was not fortune or me
Just a chapter now closed
For a new one has shown
It was meant to be
The gift is - he was able to see
Through me.

TO YOU MY FATHER

Good to know that you are around
Keeping my feet firm on the ground
You taught me well
Though I bucked your rules
At times I thought life was cruel
Now that I am middled-aged
And a sage,
Life today is but a stage
Rehearsals are over
The curtain's up
The star of the show comes into view
It is of course, You!
Director, producer, script writer too
Oh why didn't I listen to you?
I'm listening now
Like the dove of peace
For you are the eagle the wisdom I seek
The wise owl who sees all
You make me walk tall
Full of pride, but there are tears in my eyes
For a daughter should be all
I haven't been
I know that now.

Gone are the years and your birthday's here
Today is the start of a brand new sphere
Let me wish you well in heart and health
With joy in living, happiness for wealth
Let it be God's will for you to have
Many returns on this earth's plane
Paving the way for the light years left
That you my father, are eternally blessed.

LOVERS LAMENT

The journey of a lifetime
Is the ecstasy of love
Where do you go to
When you're with the one you love
The combining of two people
As they explore their bodies bare
With joy of giving into
Treasured pleasure shared
Until meeting at that kingdom
Where Loves togetherness
Is so beautiful and rare

Do not cloud the issue
With arguments on living
For when you are lovers
Your kingdoms' sweet refrain
Will see you through the jousting
For your loving will remain.

FIRST LOVE

Your vehicle came into sight
My stomach churned
My heart took flight
As you stepped from the car
I watched with glee
Because I knew you were calling for me
You closed the door tight
And walked into the night
Through the entrance
Up one flight
My doorbell rang
You were there in the light.

That was 33 years ago!

You stand before me now
A fuller figure
So proud, feet firm on the ground
Hair slightly gray
Different specs
Still that look it says regret

We were wrong
When our hearts were strong
To go in opposite directions
Our lives took us worlds apart
But in our hearts we knew
Wherever we went
Whatever we did
Respect and love grew
Through the years
We've both shed tears

Some for love lost
Some for lost years
Each time I see you
You make me feel
Your warmth and love is very real
We've never lied
Sometimes we've cried
Neither one of us need to hide the fact
That love with us didn't ride.

Here you are standing so tall
With age now I'm growing small
But my heart, like yours
Remembers the yearning
When we were young and burning
Now we have that mutual respect
With real love I do detect
For we have loved for so many years
We agreed one time
In a previous life
You and I were
Husband and wife
So it was and so shall it be
Me loving you, you loving me.

HAUNTING FLIGHT

The quilt engulfed her body, she stretched
Remembering the night's embrace
A faint smile came over her face
Tingles arose from head to toe
As she relived loves' flow
United as one in the darkness of night
Taking her on an ecstasy flight
Was this fantasy
Could this man really be
She clutched at the pillow
It smelt of he
This man was real and so was she.

Rising now to start her day
The warmth from her body seemed to say
The night has gone but through the day
Love returns in a haunting way
Thinking of when he held her tight
The caress of his lips
How they clung to become one
Hours pass
Day is night
In each others' arms
They're on that same flight!

TO KNOW LOVE

To love and be loved my aim,
Must I play the waiting game?
Doesn't happen overnight,
When it comes don't take fright,
It's here, three cheers!

It's not you fool,
You're in love with love that isn't true.
Yes it is watch the balloon
There it's popped down you drop,
There you go Doom and Gloom.

Love comes in a glow,
You didn't know
Of course when you least expect it so,
Your stomach didn't churn;
Bells didn't ring in your head,
And it wasn't what was said,
It's a feeling-a warmth, an inner peace
A calmness no one else could reach,

It's here.
How wonderful to know
Love and Love so.

PART III

WHAT'S IN A NAME

In 1967 I married
Thought t'was for life
26 years later
He has another wife

Never mind
Life you see
Turned out for the best
With a man
Same name as he
My heart has come to rest

I speak his name
With eternal pride
Enjoy warmth by his side
Feel secure in his arms
Succumb to his charms
Happiness is for me
To be in the company
Of this man with
The same name as he

LISTEN TO THE LOOK

Lulled into bliss from just one kiss?
No, this was meant to be,
Foundations now must be laid
Each day is a step to pave the way
So both can say we understand
We heard before, we talked a lot
But life, everyday living, a different pot
You forget to say please - cuddle or squeeze -
Kiss along the way.

When to talk and when to listen
Man and woman have risen
To join as one in heart and home
Not down each other and talk in drones
The teething problems are overcome
Warmth and love have just begun
And if there is a need to fight
Say your piece, make it light
End the words before the night.

That aloofness that you had before
Is no good with what's in store
Stop, Look, Listen - that's the art
You'll know before you start
There will be language of a different kind
Then you can speak of things on your mind,
The look is knowing
The ear now listens
Watch how eye's glisten
Your heart can glow - for now you know.

When man meets woman, and woman meets man
Those stares and kisses on the surface show
Now understand the depth within
Only then can love begin.
Not a new story, you stop it if you can
Man meets woman, woman meets her man!

DESTINY

We met quite by chance
Him meeting me was an avalanche
He's set in his ways by the age he has reached
Love isn't easy his past bittersweet
He is cutting, sarcastic, precise most of the time
Gets on with his life, others fall in line
His life now is not the same
But he hasn't changed
His terms or not at all
One could say that is cruel
Let's look at it overall

Freedom is within oneself
To stand your ground when friends are round
To air your views, in public too
If you so wish to do
To decline invitations
Keep one's own reservations
All of this is acceptable
For they are the rights of an individual
Nothing to do with the terms of this man
There isn't a rulebook, he didn't plan
Meeting a woman of this brand

Freedom I have cherished
Wisdom I have gained
The need for company, I have not displayed
I am, as I am,
To others I am strange
Outspoken?
Yes of course I am
Why should I sham

So now let me speak of this man
His life may well have changed
But his rules remain the same
They are based on knowledge from his past
Where sadness turned his aching heart
And mended it with hardness
At times he has an icy stare,
which makes me feel he doesn't care.
But something tells me - Don't despair.

Freedom for me has changed
It happened that wondrous night
Cupid struck
Out hearts took flight
We impressed each other beyond a doubt
Locking all others out
Our single lives are now on hold
For a man that's staid
And a woman that's bold
Rules of trust are pure gold.

UNSELFISH THOUGHTS

When at first you meet
Compliments and whispers are a treat
At times you have a view
And voice it softly to get it through
It's acceptable for a time
That's why they say
Love is blind
Opposites tend to attract
But all too soon it's an act
Discussing past love affairs
Concerned not because you care
But you need to know what went wrong
So as to avoid the same song
When at ease with the one of your dreams
You see the dangers lurking there
And want to say, but don't dare.

Your marriages, sir, were strong
But your thoughts were wrong
You're selfish, opinionated,
No room for doubt
You ask an opinion then down you shout
You don't listen to what it's about
Don't question me
I'm right you see
Until your woman wants to be free
It isn't easy give and take
A relationship is to forsake
Not only the charms of others
But giving way to your partner's thoughts and troubles
Share your views, not shout them out

There are certain things
That aren't talked about
Togetherness is very rare
It's an unselfish act
That says - You care.

INSECURITY

Best you run away with me
A joke from a friend to me
Then I felt alone
The note I had left on leaving home
Said to meet me there
We'll have a drink
Giving you time to unwind. I think

He never came
I felt a fool
Thought the man was being cruel
Telephone and see what's what
No reply, he isn't home
Working late
He could have 'phoned

Hurry back
Key in the latch
The phone rings now
He's on the line!
Hello darling, yes I'm fine!!

PRESENCE ACCEPTED

My day starts when my man departs
A kiss on the cheek and he's off

This morning was different
I could tell at a glance
And smiled in acceptance of knowing
My body outstretched
Ready to receive the warmth my man was showing
I noticed his arms how strong they'd become
His face now glowing
He seems at ease
It must be the love I am showing

He didn't know four months ago
Where or how we were going
Time has passed
I've accepted his way - give or take a day
My presence he has taken to task
But he's used to it now
And mellowed a lot
He knew from the start
Just what he had got

I'm now under his skin
And know his odd ways
Sharing part of his day
It's getting to be a part within me
Accepting his warmth willingly
With my body and mind in tune to his whims
Loving the loving he brings

RESENTMENT

A word can change one's life
If the word is love your face lights
If the word is hate friend becomes foe
If the word is resent it's time to go
That's cut and dried why waste tears
It's not as though it's been years
Still that voice inside stirs
Pack and leave - don't be absurd
But how can I stay another day
When he doesn't want it that way

Head says go, leave the key
In a day he'll forget me
Heart says stay; you'll hear him say
'Sorry' for resenting
It's fear and words hurt
One doesn't think in anger you just blurt
But this was said in a cool, calm way
So it really must mean
Go away.

Change the word
Turn the clock back
Forget the hurt - No you can't do that
Best to leave - be on your way
Maybe love will follow you - one day.

WHEN

Tomorrow is another day
Confusion may go away
You wouldn't be here
He voiced one day
If I didn't want you to stay
Two days later
Change of thought
We're not together, was the retort.

Following logic I should leave
For this man is too hard to please
I may still have to - that I know
But when the pendulum swings
And love flows
He'll know love as he has never known
I say when - not if or should
For this man really could
And when the realization happens
And this man is loving me
I wonder when it happens
Will I still be me?

A VOICE FROM ABOVE

I've packed and I'm leaving
I suddenly know
This relationship is a no go
The yearning for his love
Is making my life heavy
Still a voice from above says 'stay'
Don't throw this love away
What Love have I got
If I haven't his love
Tears now are flowing
I am not glowing
This cannot be
An emotional sea is drowning me

A pat on the head
A cuddle in bed
I look for the look
Was that for me?
Surely this is not the way
Let me go
I don't want to stay
It's hurting me this way

When walking in town
I take his arm and feel him tense
Feelings are not there
So why, oh why do I still care?

Watching him with friends of long standing
I'm on my own and not handling
The feeling that comes across
Which seems to say
You're not part of me go away!

You're certainly not here to stay
My mind clouds over
My heart just sinks
Security goes on the blink
I cannot smoke for it offends
Alcohol flows and I'm not with friends
So, on a high I try to blend
But then I see what I don't want to see
And me is not really me

I'm soft, warm, loving and true
Without feeling wanted it cannot come through
So what dear Lord what am I supposed to do
Yes I know
Unpack carry on loving
And trust in you.

HURT

Hurt deep inside
Do I run can I hide?
If I leave will I be missed?
Makes no difference
For if I leave
I'm telling me
I no longer care

He's ill right now in bed alone
I'm banished to a different zone
The front bedroom for me tonight
At times I think this man is acting
A different bed to stop the contact
Of a common cold
Maybe he's getting old
After all last night's love
When it did unfold
Went through to the early hours

Shouldn't feel this way
Should let him sleep alone and say
Have a good nights rest
When dawn breaks be at your best
Can't say that because you see
Actually he doesn't like me

Hurt, hurt inside
Maybe it's foolish pride
No! I am hurt
Hurt deep inside
Instinct tells me
This man has lied

WARM

Warm, come into the warm
The first line of a song
Sent by a man, I had not known long
Believing the sentiment to be true
I wallowed and thought of pastures new

Dining, dancing, romancing what bliss
To be held in the arms of this man and be kissed
Caring and sharing
As lovers delight
With tender caresses and warmth through the night

I took the line of warmth and love
Cooed for a while
Like a collared dove
Back off came the order, Try to blend
Curtail kisses and cuddles
In other words, do not apprehend

Once warmth and love inside was showing
My face was glowing
Now I look in the mirror
I see, a me, that is not allowed to be me
Is it wrong to demonstrate?
Show feelings - love or hate

My feelings were there, growing
Now they have gone, that I am knowing
For you will not allow me to care
And you're far too selfish to share
Warm, come into the warm
What warm? It's cold in there.

ABANDONED

The store was closing
Doors were being locked
Where was he
I went into shock
Stay here said he
Won't be a sec, have to get something from outside
That was 20 minutes ago
The knot in my stomach doubled
Many years before
I was abandoned in a store.

An ice-cold wind hit my face
To the car park I raced
To face his car minus him
Life was looking very grim
Where was my trust
Why had it gone
The conversation was wrong
Before we entered that awful store
Our relationship was on the floor
I knew that morning
He was in a huff
I didn't conform enough

When meeting his friends
Hush and blend
How can I when he doesn't extend
Warmth I can respond to
I would sit and listen
To them reminiscing
Delight in hearing the past
But somehow or other

They huddle together
I'm not made to feel a part
Now I'm wandering around
With my head in a whirl
Remembering bitterness past
I think I'll stand still
And just let the chill
Go out of my aching heart
Standing quite numb
He comes into view
To his eye there's nothing wrong
But a second look shows
My eyes are in shock
I'm not moving from head to my toes

He now knows what's wrong
Is upset to think
My thoughts of him
Were so low
He hadn't gone far
Just to the hotel
To acquire a room for the night
He talked it all through
We've discussed us before
This time was different for me
A woman of strength
Reduced to a wimp
From insecurity

He's not caring for me
I'm living a lie or maybe a dream
I was abandoned before
And walked for miles
They found me a heap in the snow

I couldn't talk then
It's difficult now
How is this man then to know
Forget it, he's not interested in you
Leave whilst you've still got some faith
It's not like before
Walk out the door
Do it before your heart breaks.

WARMTH FROZE

Like a chilling dart
Piercing my heart
In an instant
Feelings died
His ice-cold stare
Stripped me bare
Of the warmth
I felt inside

Once I was held
And made to know
That, that kiss meant
I want you so
Just thinking of him
Made me glow
But with that stare
My heart froze
I feel I no longer care
How can I now,
With the cold emptiness there.

DWELL IN A DREAM

Oh how lovely in all it's splendor
A sight I shall remember
Proud, alluring all alone
Silently I groaned
For there you were in front of me
A dream.

Fleetingly I caught a glimpse
Grey stone walls with shapes so rare
Your roof a dying art
I'll never know what's beyond your path
But that glimpse went to my heart

In you house, I would like to live
And really get to know
You are my dream
Dreams aren't lived in
They simply come and go

HOME

Home - where is home?
Where the heart is some would say
What if you part
And your heart is lost
Where does it dwell,
In a wishing well?
Where can it stay,
If it can't find it's way?
Where does love go
When it hasn't a home?

PART IV

TALK
Relationships can be cruel
But at their best put to the test
They're the ones to build on
To be able to talk
To enjoy the delights
Of mental and physical attraction
If that comes through
Your relationship is true
For those built on fairy tales
Are very thin in depth

But to talk it through
To feel the need
To voice what is wrong
To them embrace
With warmth and love
Nothing is so strong

LOOK OF CHANGE

Man meets woman, woman meets man
Not a new story, stop it if you can
There is a look, aloof they say
Coldness can be classed that way.
On the rare occasion, the look can change
That haunting stare can rearrange
A heart that once was deranged
But what's it for this lull into bliss
Will it lead to happiness?
Your eyes have met
Your lips have kissed
You've felt the caress of his finger tips
You've listened and learnt when not to speak
The beginning tastes so sweet.

Time moves on, man has his mate
The talking with is not so great
Listening too becomes a bore
Before you know, there's an uproar
All too soon one retreats
And says this situation will not repeat.
It does in time, when you see that stare
You know your heart is going to care.
When it does remember this:
Share a lover's tiff
It takes two to come adrift
One not talking, the other no ears
There's no time factor it doesn't take years
It's all to do with talking to
There is a way, that makes listening a joy,
To be spoken to - talked with - music to the ear
When lectured . . . Cloth ears.

PASSED BY

To love and be loved is my aim
Must I play the waiting game?
Years have passed, times been wasted

People say don't be hasty
How long does it take
To find one's mate
How many times can the heart break?
The sun goes down
The dawn breaks
One hears the chorus of the birds and awakes
Joy would be to turn and hold
Nuzzle close
Feel the warmth unfold
True love is never cold

To love and be loved was my aim
I tried again and again
Now I'm old and passed yearning
The sun's gone down
No longer burning

FEELINGS STIRRED

Why this yearning - these thoughts
A strong lady self-taught
Many a time my heart has stirred,
the mind has said "DON'T BE ABSURD"
Remember the pain from the lover's dart
Think with your head, forget your heart.

Time will heal, children will warm
"ARE YOU SURE?" I sat and said
"Yes" replied the expert (for he's well read)
An animal, a babe in arms
You'll soften, give way to charms
Never happened, never aglow
Where did my feelings go?
Here they are, stirring now
When I have no wish to bare, even less to care
Never known trust, Survival that is me
Riding the waves of the human sea.

But I can't ignore the feeling I saw
Or how my heart locked into place,
Suddenly starting to race.
The more he talked, I felt a longing
In a way, a sense of belonging.

Now this yearning - these thoughts
Ludicrous for a strong lady self-taught
Life brings wisdom,
You're a canny cat
Your know just where you're at
Take a bow lady now,
Your head and heart are one
Let it flow, be aglow, wallow in this bliss

OH HEAD! OH HEART! DON'T EVER PART
HOW I LONG FOR HIS KISS.

A GLINT

Eyes are the windows of your soul
Mine are brown in color, dark as coal
Sadness shows - tears have flowed
They have wept for years
A deep regret that love hasn't entered yet
Excited yes
Like a child at play
When they think love is coming their way
They glint like candles in the night
Candles burn out - was there a light?

TEARS

Tears will they ever stop
Here they come
Drop, drop, drop
The past tears have been of fear
These tears the future
Near and dear
On the brink
I dare not think
Down they come
Blink, blink, blink.

Tears of joy just may happen
If he loved me
They would be
If he can't
Then never
My heart locked forever

Tears - oh no
Make my heart glow
Look my way
Let them flow
For this man to see
In love with him forever
I will be

DO YOU REMEMBER

What a shame
Not to be involved
In collecting items
Where stories can be told
Of do you remember when
We saw this picture of this hen
And had to buy it for our kitchen
Then we.......

What's the point?
Marriages later
Boxes of memories
Shackles galore
Asking friends
Can they store
Your treasured joys
While you mend your heart
Forgetting which part
You put in a box somewhere

Is it any wonder
That you hear thunder,
When you venture to trust yet again?
She walks down the street
Sees something sweet
Looks up with big eyes and then
You look down at the face
That you want to embrace
And a voice in your head
Says "Stop"
Remember the boxes
The memories there

You shake your head
She lowers her eyes
It comes as little surprise
She has boxes of her own

No one's to blame
You say 'won't happen again'
But collecting together is fun
You're accepting each other
So trust in the new

Bury those boxes and be one!

CHRISTMAS SHARING

Tonight is the start of Christmas Fayre
It's new for me to share
Christmas past has been alone
I really haven't cared
It's nice to have you by my side
This Yule tide

Merry Christmas, Happy New Year
All the things for good cheer
Joy and good fortune is my wish for you
May your dreams be fulfilled, your problems few
Either way it's nice being with you.

PART V

FAITH

Home is the size of a postage stamp
1st class is best
I'm rich in mind, I tell myself

Leaving the materialistic world to fend for itself
For it doesn't seem to provide for me
Thus causing uncertainty

Love to have you at the fayre
But you can't afford to pay your share
I'll pay as I go was my defense
Can't have that. You must pay for hire
Oh well! Hang fire
I'll get there - just you see
For I have faith in penniless me!

AWAKENING

The phone rings
My heart sings
Your voice is joy to my ear
I hold you so very dear
You're in my heart
You're in my head
So, of course
You're in my bed.

To lie with you
To feel your touch
My body yearning
For your love, so much
You've kindled
Feelings inside me
I never thought that that could be
Sometimes tears of joy are inside me
You make me feel so womanly
Your tender care
Your strength - so rare
Your icy stare - that says
Don't you dare

I know how far I can go
To the bitter sweet
To the love complete
To the warmth of you
That makes me sweet
To your open arms
To your wonderful charms
To the strength of a man
Who makes no demands

THOUGHT

Absence makes the heart grow fonder
Out of sight, makes it colder
Time goes on
You're a lot older!

UPLIFTED

The phone rings
The birds sing
The sun is shining
I am gliding, on a wing
For now my heart has
Taken flight and in his
Arms I will be tonight.

MATERIALISM

Silks and satins
Diamonds - waste
Emeralds to ward off
Jealousy that's always chased
Decisions often made in haste
Buy this, buy that
Because you can - was "that" the plan?
No! You lost the plot.........
Love is something you cannot purchase
It has no price, but it holds you warm
And sparkles like the golden dawn.

Let things go, reach for that star
One more time - it's there, it's not far
Ride, on the crest of the wave
Don't be a slave to materialism
Working yourself into the ground
Turn around "look" what you've found
That star's so bright it shines all night
It's yours to hold, it's yours to take
Grab it for goodness sake

Sink or swim, do your own thing
Find what love and loving can bring
Money can buy sparkly things
But that star in the sky.......
Money cannot buy, because it harbors
Priceless things
It tells a story of love's sweet glory
Way beyond your wildest dreams
I'm reaching up to you my star
I am ready now, to go where you are.

MELTING

Ecstasy, when this man enters me
I feel his warmth, I feel his love
I want to give, can't get enough
Why is this so?

The way he talks, as though he knows
Love within froze
I've been on ice, it wasn't nice
He has the key, to the real me,
I never dreamt
That a man like this, would want to be with me

The time of tide within me shows hurt
But my heart has soared
Hurt will deplete
FOR I AM - NOW COMPLETE

HELLO YOU

Never lovers - ever friends
Rash statement can it never bend
Catch a star, see a moon beam
Blind is love
I've held that star, seen that beam
Life isn't what it seems.

Never lovers - ever friends
No! That's life's story at an end
For friends are lovers learning to blend
If not in body, then in mind
Somewhere, somehow that clock does chime
You strike a cord of mutual trust
Lovers and friends are life's must

To be a friend and a lover too
How nice to meet
Hello to you.

HARMONY

He's as tall as a tree
Strong like oak
But he sees all things
From root to breeze
Nothing escapes the leaves
On his tree

He is all knowing
For that I'm glowing
How wise is he - in his oak tree

He's been uprooted
Not disputed
He saw a willow
That was fate
He took the willow, as his mate

His back is hard
His exterior gruff
That's because life's been rough
He's weathered many a storm
Now the sun can make him warm
For the willow's strong
She bends to flow 'caressing' water
So she can grow

The oak will shield
The willow will yield
The oak will lead
The willow will reed
Harmony

JEWEL

Precious! Precious!
A first for me
How lovely - to be
What an endearment
From thee

MISSING LOVING

I miss you, that's all I can say
Love comes in a funny way
I love you, an emotion
Showing one's devotion
Why do I feel the need to express it
When I never knew, that I possessed it
How strange life can be
It's certainly altered me.

I miss you, that's all I can say
But I have never missed before
Not in this way
Loves and losses have come my way
I've trained myself, to steer away
From loves hurt

Love comes but once, so they say
I'm more fortunate than most,
Twice it came my way
One I adored, and still have pain
The other a sweet refrain, the tables turned
I'm his old flame, neither of which
I have never missed, not in this way.

Perhaps this is real, perhaps it's not
I know one thing, I don't want it to stop
If missing is loving, and loving is kissing
And yearning is burning with desire untouched
Then I'm missing the loving, and I'm loving
The missing for I'm yearning for the time
When I can feel his touch, see his eyes blue
And sparkling, his smile so encouraging his arms

Open wide to engulf me inside,
Methinks I'm loving the loving
And loving the love
I'm responding to loving
So therefore I love!

VOILA!

Once upon an afternoon
25th of May, not June
This man came into view
I was so astonished, that it was you
A man I had met at a party, yet,
I did regret, I was married at the time
For I wanted more of his mind and chatter
Everything he said, seemed to matter.

Marriage of convenience I had done
And ended up without any fun
I could have been
Left without funds
I pulled the rug, and off he did run

Now sitting at the French Café
Very pleased with the events of the day
There he was in all his glory
Did he remember me, did he know the story
He smiled, we chatted, I felt the same
This man had a brain

Now he's brought me alive, I'm all aflame
Oh Lord! I hope it's not a game
We're into June, three weeks on
My heart now singing a different song
I'm all aglow and all a dither
Selling up, starting a new,
I must be one of the chosen few
For love has blossomed with you
Once upon a time in June

A BREEZE

For a brief moment my eyes shone
My heart was singing a love song
A close encounter of the loving kind
Up I soared, oh so blind
On what I can only call a dream ride
The dream has shattered, there was bliss
I did feel magic in his kiss
Not to be, he didn't love me
He was my dream
But he wasn't for me!

COLD MEMORIES

My heart is cold
I'm growing old
Look my hair's gone gray
Living now from day to day
On memories

Out of sight, out of mind
Leave foolishness behind
Watch young lovers, as they dream
Remember once, you loved and dreamed
Now you're awake, your heart did break
And there's no one now it seems

It isn't age that stopped you loving
Just the thought of that awful longing
That aching pain of a heavy heart
When lovers have to part
It's never mutual, there's always hurt
Live with your memories, don't divert
Remember the love you had
Before it went so very bad!

LOVE

Love of my life
Light of my love
You have me cooing
Like a turtle dove

Tragic life past, future aglow
Because it is you I have come to know
To accept your love
With sweet return
Never again to yearn
For here we are
With a love so true
My darling how I love you!

FRIEND

What is a friend?
What do they demand?
Your time, having a birthday card?

How do you know when a friend is true
It's trust one feels, from them to you
To share life's laughter.
The tears as well, and know with both
They wish you well.

To call and know they're there for you
That's a friend and one that's true
Such a friend I have found in you.

THINK BEFORE YOU SPEAK

Waiting, wanting, not knowing
If this love will work
Once I sat and thought it's growing
Oh why should love hurt?
Why does that bubble always burst?

Inside I know that this can work
If I put aside my hurt
This love is real
I know I feel
If only I could show it
Things I say, are said the wrong way
So of course I blow it

Trust in time, it never fails
Don't put love on the scales
This was fate, it will be great
Just speak with a different sound.

OLD FLAME

Sitting here with pen in hand
Wondering what I'll write
Will it be what's in my heart
Or what is in my sight.

The man I see is not what was
He's changed so much with time
Passed his prime - staid
Love in him is cold.

Love in me is burning bright
Together we will share the light
For I will kindle that man to warmth
That burns - long into the night.

THE END IS THE BEGINNING

Loving him hurt me a lot
My heart died, how I cried
Dreams shattered, nothing mattered
Inside me, love shattered.

Absence makes the heart grow fonder, so they say,
But I did wonder
We had our breaks, months at a time
Still our love didn't rhyme
Then I left - went overseas
Taking with me, shattered dreams
Building a life from place to place
Not looking at men face to face
I knew in my heart, we had to part
Never again would I feel love
Held with warmth from dusk to dawn
Burning with pride when by his side
Yearning to hear what he felt inside.

I never knew what fate had in store
For it returned me, to these shores
To find him here with open arms, waiting with love in full command
Wanting the dreams of long ago
Opening his heart, his eyes aglow
Putting to rights the wrongs that had hurt
Making me know, love inside him flowed
Not fearing voicing those magical words and demanding
My answer - if my heart still yearned
It didn't take long for me to know, those tears of hurt of long ago.

ALONE

Hour after hour time ticks by
Sleep how it eludes me
Sitting in an uncomfortable chair
Was that footsteps on the stair
Not for me, no visitors here, loneliness.

How dark the night
Days go by, no one in sight
Bedsit land, one room to dwell
A single bed, a living hell

No need for shackles to complicate life
Rent a room say goodnight -
To whom do you communicate?
Yourself, one room, doom and gloom

Nights are long

Days unfilled
Listen the telephone's ringing
A chat to a friend
Please don't ring off
I need to talk to a human being!

HURT

People don't realize what they say
How hurt I am, for another day
When will hurt go away
I didn't choose to live this way - circumstances
A lesson learnt
Make roots, don't take chances
On offshoots

So here I am and judgment's passed
For finances are nil, and money's class
How shallow people are, so quick to
Down and wear a frown - stating
How did you get to where you are?
Heart rules,
Head was lost
Just clown faced
Full of zest
Work from home someone suggests.

LOVEBIRDS

I wondered why the garden
Was full of flurry
Tits, finches, robins and sparrows
Picking up nuts in a hurry
Birds to and fro
They knew it would snow
The collared doves
Regular visitors
They sit on the fence and coo
Waiting for nuts to drop from above
Their beaks are too big for the box

They know that I am watching
That my door will open
And a handful of nuts will be thrown
They swoop down, collect and go home
The male ever watchful
Close to his dove
The female cosseted
Under the wings of his love
Not unlike humans I would say
Except that doves show it
In a nicer way

LOVE IS CARING AND SHARING
WHEN
TWO HEARTS BEAT AS ONE
GIVING AND LOVING IS LIVING
FULFILLMENT OF LIFE
HAS BEGUN

www.ingramcontent.com/pod-product-compliance
Lightning Source LLC
Chambersburg PA
CBHW061502040426
42450CB00008B/1451